Advice for Travelers
& other poems

AILEEN BASSIS

Published by Black Sunflowers Poetry Press
www.blacksunflowerspoetry.com

© Aileen Bassis 2024

ISBN: 978-1-7396267-5-4

All rights reserved

for Andrew

Table of Contents

Summer Saturday on Fourth Street	1
Alternative Questions for New Citizens	3
I Fit My Life Into a Small Suitcase	4
The Bear is Not Dreaming	5
For the Ruined	6
Potters Field	8
Advice For Travelers	9
Sundered	10
America in 2022	11
Winter Begins in Berlin	12
Sur Le Pont	14
Luncheon in Lagrasse	15
The Last Time I Saw Karina	17
The Medieval Artist Pauses	18
The Girl She Used To Be	19
The Light's About to Change	20
Someday is Today	21
Acknowledgements	23

Summer Saturday on Fourth Street

the singer cried out, it's the end of the world song

every one roared   yeah

on their feet, drinking beer,
fist bumps, a brush-stroked snare drum
    welcome end of the world

      welcome twenty-first century

and sun-hat wearing babies
who may open their nonagenarian eyelids
to another century's reel

maybe their world will end
        dancing
    welcome
as a sun-glazed drunk
who bandy-legged
sways in synching rhythm,
hooked by a maenad's seaweed-colored hair
damp against her hot pink shirt and tattoos rushing
along her thighs and up a rotund rollicking ass

    welcome
frolic panegyric to summer flesh
festooned in dandelion, coral and grape
glitter skirting pale forearms blushing rose,
legs browning, drowned
in the fathomless dark of oiled bellies

    welcome
arcane anarchy overflowing
in rhyme or song imploding

the drumbeat's calculus, parsing
time's incremental tap-steps

one, two, and four

Alternative Questions for New Citizens

Will this country dress you in its history
and braid stories in your hair?

Can you put happiness under your pillow
and have it sleep beside your feet?

Is a future waiting on the other side
of every door?

Can freedom keep you warm or is it
light as drifting mist so you
never see where it ends and how
the sky begins?

I Fit My Life into A Small Suitcase

(Tatiana Bolidanova, from NY Times, April 19, 2022)

What can else can be inside?
— the familiar comfort of clean socks
or a flash drive in case the cloud can't be found
& papers that may tumble into a puddle & then
you're left without proof of who you are
or where you're from in a foreign land
& will your suitcase hold the smell of boiling
food that swept the hall each evening
or dust motes swirling as you pulled
the curtain open to welcome your artless
gaze & what will next week or month
reveal as each hour unfolds its creases
& crumpled stains that you rub & rub
& spit & rub again

The Bear Is Not Dreaming

Pushing aside a bottle on the table
and tearing off a piece of bread,
there's a whisper, *Maybe*
the bear wakes again.

A rank smell enters the room.
The bear swings a heavy
leg over a door sill,

floorboards gasp.

The bear's body fills the room.
Hunger turns his glassy blue
eye a colder shade.

His breath burns like ice.
His gravelly voice,
crackles like a late-night
radio broadcast cutting in
and out while a careening Lada thumps
down the H15 to Donetsk.

Cousins,
he lifts a thick nailed paw,
always, we were one.

For the Ruined

you can't
imagine buildings
collapsing: sofa cushions,
curtain shreds, window
glass, sheaves of plaster-
board flooding
streets or imagine sky
shrilling into yellow
with a burst that's
longer than a breath
and bites through closed
eyelids and you don't
want to imagine
blood's brilliant flower
dimming into other shades
— from a bitten plum
mouth
to a softening hue
from light leaving
to red-black
quivering like an iris
in an open eye —
you can't think

of the odors

that won't carry any words

at all

or how each body lies—

Potters Field

Some say the name's from the Aramaic, "a field of blood" and others say potters were wanderers, vagrants, rootless ones, the dispossessed and friendless.

There are videos of crews there in white hazmat suits, digging furrows for coffins. Three deep, row after row. Bodies in white boxes that will mix with remains of still-born babes, with bones of the poor who died from yellow fever and Spanish flu. With AIDS victims who may have walked past me on New York streets in bodies flush with possibility. Now they all mingle in brown dirt, claimed by tree roots and beetles and mindless foraging ants. And as for the island that holds this Potters Field? It's named Hart Island. Not named "heart" for the organ beating beneath the ribs but "hart," a name for a male deer.

A name for an island shaped like a deer leg. A flattened haunch ending in a solitary spit, reminiscent of a black cloven hoof that can bear a body as it walks.

Advice for Travelers

When you leave your country, put your papers
        in a plastic bag, then zip it shut.
When you leave your country, hide money
        in your shoe or in your underwear.
When you leave, put crackers in your pocket
        and an extra shoelace too.
And you better know how to swim and be ready
        to walk all day.
Learn to say "when" and "why." Learn how to move
        your tongue. Learn how to shape your lips.
Remember a blanket when you leave,
        for nowhere will be soft.
When you leave your country, your thoughts will
        sift like flour through a sieve. And when
you leave your country, your name may curl
        inside your ribs and tap like insects
        on a windowpane at night.
Leave your country and you'll find rooms and streets
        of children, but they may not be your own.
When you leave, you may study your open palm
        and wonder if any future's hiding there.
When you leave, you may even lose your
        body and then what becomes of you?
Leave, and you may find that no one tells the truth
        and truth is sitting on a chair that wobbles on three legs.
And even after you leave, your country's hard
        and stubborn, a tiny seed stuck
        between your teeth
And you can't tell if the taste is bitter or if
        you're tasting something sweet.

Sundered

wind is blowing
from the north
from the west

unseen fires are burning
and your hair your
hair
smells of smoke

scatter salt
spill sugar
for here
is the wayward path of insects:
small flying things they
flutter past
leaving brown stains on your
sleeve

I looked for echoes of
another
in your words but found
lizards
and snakes and crumbs on a
stone
terrace while you swallow
feathers
and bloody beaks whole and
ask
forgiveness for what's ahead.

America in 2022

guns in closets
under beds
guns in drawers and guns
in dashboard glove compartments
there are guns tucked into waistbands and rifles
stored in lockers and automatics kept
locked with muzzles pointing down
and guns with steel barrels and heated
metal hammers and main springs
and front sights and rear sights
and cylinder metal clips
there are ghost guns made from online kits
and boxes filled with bullets and loaded
magazines at the ready and rifles cradled
against shoulders that are ready for a kick
and don't forget
fingers to pull a trigger
and hands to fold around the grip
eyes to find their target
and minds to have the will.

Winter Begins in Berlin

Wilhelm Müller, "Die Winterreise"

And when the cock crowed
My eyes opened;
it was cold and dark,
And the ravens croaked from the rooftops.

I've been coughing ever since
I came to Berlin, where
I stand to eat currywurst, dripping red
sauce on my shoe,
and the smell of burning
sausage is mixed with cigarette smoke
blurring crowds outside bars,

where U-Bahn cars screech above stunted
trees reaching up to a dimming sky,
where afternoon grows colder
until night pulls a tight grey stocking
over layers of baroque buildings;
an old world panoply of insouciant
parlors and vacant cellars,

where a wrinkled world spews
a scribbled palimpsest onto emptying streets
and one green light blinks *Apotheke,*
where a honeyed tenor voice drips Schubert's
Die Winterreise from an iPod player
beside a clerk, her copper eyes
glinting like pfennigs lost
in powdered snow.

She hands
me a bottle that reeks of ivy
leaf and pine mold with a label
that I can't read, and all that Berlin
night, I'm waking to hear winter crows
and sipping syrup from a tiny
stolen spoon.

Sur Le Pont

Trying
to understand each other now
is a sojourn at a foreign movie.

Maybe
I need new
glasses because the subtitles
are hard to read; words just
disappear, but
     it doesn't matter
precisely what anyone is saying, because
I can see love
and evasion,
arguments and despair.

If only there was a crazed
car chase or explosion to burst
with adrenaline instead of glances
in black and white
framed in cigarette smoke.

I hear sax chords shift and I know
that means something bad is coming
but maybe, after all, it doesn't
matter because *LE FIN* scrolls
across the screen.

     Couldn't you see
the girl in a checked coat dancing
on the bridge between heaps of melting
snow? and in the background of the shot,
a boat floats by. *L'on y danse,*
        l'on y danse.

Luncheon in Lagrasse

a friday afternoon in may
with redolent peaches resting on blue,
as words ping-pong from german
to english to spanish to french,
talking real estate prices, divorces,
revolutions,

and one guest explains,
i'm english, not british, part spanish
too, people see my big nose, they guess
i'm a jew, and another adds,
there was freud, and their music,
so much to like, and yiddish
is like german,

and he recalls when his mutter
called hitler a fool, but then,
who could believe what was
going to happen, but no,
we all knew what
was going to happen, and he
slices up sausages, sweating pearls
of white fat and another exclaims
who can understand
scots, and the normans,
the bretons, one-hundred year war,

the french said, don't worry, we hate
the brits more than the krauts, and she
squeezed some pate on a round of white bread
recalling, we tried to escape
on a boat on a lake but the swiss
turned us back,
they do like their rules, and wait,

here's dessert,
goat cheese on a tray with espresso
in neat little cups,
and i notice a bitten swiss chocolate
staining the red and pink linen

while the mistral (it's occitan for idiot
wind) tugs the cloth and motorcycles
rush by wearing helmets like bullets,
très chic in their leather, and we all kiss
good-bye, not once, we kiss twice, saying
it's been just delightful, it's all been delightful,
so very nice.

The Last Time I Saw Karina

music slips restless fingers into pockets of conversation as we listen
to Karina speak without a pause/ her pale-egg face crushed beneath
black hair streaming away like her kiss that missed my cheek/
I recall a portrait I've seen many times by the painter Soutine/
a woman in red/ coat sliced open/ fingers meeting in a nervous
steeple/ not really listening/ I imagine Soutine's village in Europe's
east before the war/ shrouded in birches/ peat smoke everywhere/
each night plowed into another day/ life chewed like black bread
until Soutine was lost in the Holocaust/ and through our entrees
and dessert/ Karina tangles streets in cities she's never seen/ her
grandmother's house in Warsaw/ a shop in Toulouse/ the Lisbon
embassy where her father waited for visas to escape/ she mixes
stories with her list of ailments/ stomach troubles/ fitful nights/
foggy thoughts / she can't remember the number on the house in
France/ and were ten cousins lost or twelve/ and where did her
mother's sisters go/ she sips some wine / declares she shouldn't
drink with all her meds/ grabs her husband's cane to walk to the
ladies room/ limping/ first with her right leg/ then dragging her
left/ turns back to tell us that gluten makes her ill or maybe it's the
new pills or a virus without a name/ she showers crumbs through
this dining maze of high-top stools and stony tables/ I hear the
music change to a wail with pounding beat / I'm tired/ I want
to leave and beckon to the waiter who extends an arm tattooed with
a scroll of dripping daggers/ his lips part / white teeth gleaming
and he bows before us like a supplicant without a prayer to ask/

17

The Medieval Artist Pauses

I should put Death in this
picture but I don't see
him as an angel, alabaster,
polished to a gleam.

Death could be a lout
in a Flanders tavern,
drunk, asleep,
then he stands up with a belch,

a scratch, walks to the fire,
pulls out his cock and pisses
over all. The smoke
is foul. He farts.

One whistle, a dog groans
and curls tight
beneath the table. Death puts
a randy hand up a slattern's skirt,

a seed shrivels in her womb.

He leaves the door ajar, dust
whirls in. A dog sneezes, then
whimpers as he dreams.

The Girl She Used To Be

Once she longed for a drawer filled with every color.
Once she stole a toy ring and chewed its plastic nub.
Once her dreams were motionless as summer heat.
Once she walked through an empty lot to train tracks
disappearing along the road and she
didn't know why they went or how
crushed weeds gathered clouds
into her mind and she crossed
avenues twisted into shapes
that had no tongues and she never told
about the stairwell or who was waiting there
and she never coiled tight inside a sound
that was just for her but found
herself in a window's dust at night
when the curtains twitched
alive and whispered — stay awake.
She wanted to be breath between a window
shade and a pane of glass
and smelled a curtain
of cooking oil and mildew
but couldn't read the tile flooring's dots
or messages in the dirt that crept
into each corner while a feeling
that she couldn't name slid inside
her like two arms
pushing into sleeves
and when her body
thickened like a package wrapped
to be sent somewhere far away
she clenched her teeth and tried
to shed her bones and muscles
and turn to steam
hissing in the pipes.

The Light's About to Change

Trying to make it across the street
before the countdown light reaches

zero, an old sock slips beneath
your heel and while bending to pull

it up, your handbag tumbles
open, spilling a welter of crumpled

store receipts, coins, and a shopping
list that sinks into a puddle

with yellow and brown wet
leaves and the list gives a single

desultory wave as ink runs
into a blur, and to a slap of beats

blaring from an open window,
a car stops short, the driver turning

to tap on a screen, and you imagine
yourself glimpsed in a camera's eye,

a pan shot up past street signs and tree
limbs to glass-box buildings

pressed to back-drop blue,
then gliding smoothly into another storyline,

while the woman in the intersection
is translucent as a negative,

a bit player in a scene
that may not make the final cut.

Someday is Today

Someday holds afternoons as gentle as an earlobe
with fingers that rain on glass and presses

one cheek to the cold

and someday will tap, no, ring

doorbells like a pillow spilling feathers

into the air and someday this old world
will sink beneath the damp squeeze of new

and a scoop of sun will shimmy into
the sky determined as a small-hipped girl

wedged into a corner seat beside

a man, overflowing and generous
as the morning until someday presses out

the hour like toothpaste on your brush to meet

today waving its pink pale star hello and rummaging

in your pocket for cookie crumbs and treats.

Acknowledgements

Summer Saturday on Fourth Street was first published in *The Seventh Quarry Poetry*, Issue Twenty-Three, Winter/Spring 2016

I Fit My Life into a Small Suitcase was first published in *Plainsongs,* Spring/Summer 2023

The Bear is Not Dreaming was first published in *New Verse News*, Jan. 2015

Potters Field, was first published in *The Southampton Review Online,* Oct. 2021

Advice for Travelers has been published in *From Everywhere A Little,* A Migration Anthology, Waters Edge Press, 2019 and with images in *Unlikely Stories*, Sept. 2022

America in 2022 was first published in *Washington Square Review* LLC, Summer 2023

Winter Begins in Berlin was first published in *Apeiron Review,* 2014

Sur le Pont was first published in *Red Branch Journal,* Spring 2014

Luncheon in Lagrasse was first published in *Stone Canoe*, 2016

The Last Time I Saw Karina, was first published in *Escape Wheel, Great Weather for Media*, 2020

The Medieval Artist Pauses was first published in *B O D Y Literature,* Sept. 2014

The Girl She Used to Be was first published in *Roanoke Review*, 2020

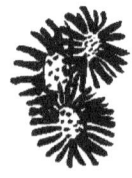

blacksunflowerspoetrypress.com

www.ingramcontent.com/pod-product-compliance
Lightning Source LLC
Chambersburg PA
CBHW040639100526

44585CB00039B/2873